1

Introduction

Introduction

The life of a Sugar Baby is limitless. Money, clothes, holidays, cars and houses, all gifted in exchange for time. For many, it sounds like a dream, or a scam, but for some girls (and guys!) this has become reality. And in this modern world of equality, why shouldn't we seek a more "mutually beneficial" relationship in our lives?

Whether you want the whole shebang, a bit of pocket money, or you're just plain curious, this book will give you the lowdown of what it takes to become a Sugar Baby. Starting with the basics – what is a Sugar Baby? Through to finding a Sugar Daddy and having a relationship.

My story is that I'm an ex-Sugar Baby, having lived the lifestyle for many years and having a number of Sugar Daddies. I have now retired from the Sugar lifestyle and am in a long-term relationship. When I first started on my Sugar journey, I found it was a guessing game to get the results I wanted, so I have written this guide to help new Sugar Babies on their quest to find their Sugar Daddy.

What is a Sugar Baby/Sugar daddy?

So what exactly is a Sugar Baby? Well, in its basic terms it is someone who is in a 'mutually beneficial' relationship with someone who can provide them with something they want/need in exchange for spending time with them.

Now, obviously this is quite vague, but in reality the types of relationships can range from having a phone call every few weeks in exchange for a bit of pocket money, to living with someone who can provide you with everything you desire, then there's a whole spectrum in between. Probably the most common scenario is dating a few times a

month in exchange for money/gifts, and this
the draw for most people considering the
Sugar baby lifestyle.

Why become a Sugar baby?

There are a number of benefits to becoming a Sugar Baby; the first and foremost reason is for financial reasons. Whether you are a student that wants tuition covered, needing a mortgage to be paid, or you just want a bit more cash to splash each month, then getting a Sugar Daddy is one way of covering this.

Similarly, a Sugar Daddy can provide gifts to a Sugar Baby, whether expensive jewellery or practical home wares. Gifting makes the relationship seem less of a transaction.

Sugar Daddies are usually high earners and have a good career behind them, with experiences in certain fields. Some Sugar Babies seek career advice, or mentorship from their Sugar Daddies to help them move forward in their own careers or businesses.

Similarly to this, Sugar Daddies usually have lifestyles that can provide a better level of experience, expensive restaurants, exotic holidays, sold-out tickets. Experiences that, sometimes, our money can't buy.

The final reason for becoming a Sugar Baby is for companionship. Sometimes you don't want to be in a traditional relationship, but it doesn't mean you don't want to go on dates or enjoy someone else's company, the Sugar Daddy relationship can just 'work' better for some people at certain times of life.

I first began my sugar journey when I felt stuck in a rut in life. I was bored of routine and just wanted a bit of excitement. I wasn't in a relationship and didn't want to be, but I still wanted companionship. I was working, but not in a secure job and certainly not earning very much. After reading a few articles about Sugar Daddies I though 'why not?' and my journey began.

Why do men become Sugar Daddies?

Companionship is the name of the game for most Sugar Daddies. Men with high flying careers, high stress and who are high profile sometimes want an escape, which is what a sugar baby can provide. For some men, their life does not allow them time for a 'traditional' relationship, so by entering a sugar relationship he is able to have the companionship without the time commitments.

For some men, the idea of marriage and family life can leave them a bit bored. Sometimes they don't get the attention they crave at home when a marriage reaches a certain point. Not wanting to leave the family or the marriage, it is sometimes a better option for them to get the attention they want elsewhere, with a Sugar Baby, escapism for a moment before returning to 'real' life.

The Sugar Daddies that I have met and dated have fit into the realms of cash rich, time poor. Having demanding, high paying jobs, but not fully getting the chance to enjoy their spoils. Some were married, passing their wives like ships in the night, living two separate lives. Some were single and unable to commit the time to a real relationship. What they all had in common was craving companionship, the company of a young woman to make them feel special, feel alive again.

CHAPTER 2

Becoming a Sugar Baby

What do YOU want out of it?

So you've read the reasons why people become Sugar Babies and the potential benefits that can be reaped, but before you get started on your sugar journey you've first got to decide what exactly you want out of it. After all this is a 'mutually beneficial' relationship, so you need to know what you want to benefit from it, what are your expectations? Once you know what it is, then you can start the search for the Sugar Daddy to suit you.

You've also got to think about the level of commitment you can offer, for instance do you have a full time career, or children, which means that spare time is limited for you? Are you able to meet up with someone at last minute, or do you have to book time well in advance? Do you want to keep the relationship discrete?

If you know what you want and what you can offer, then you will make find the right person a lot easier.

When I started out I was open to all sorts of arrangements, I liked the idea of allowances and gifts to help keep me going alongside my low paying job. But I also wanted companionship on a different level, with someone who could give me different experience. I got to go to top restaurants, amazing clubs, tickets to sold out events and trips to unbelievable locations. Over the years my priorities changed, so I chose Sugar Daddies who could provide what I needed at that time. I found the hardest thing when starting out was knowing my value and having the guts to ask for what I wanted. At the end of the day the Sugar Daddy will know the score and knows he will have to deliver.

Where to find a Sugar Daddy

Once you've decided exactly what it is you want, then the search for your Sugar Daddy can begin. For some people going out and about, visiting bars and events with high profile men to meet face to face works a dream. The problem with this is knowing which men are even interested in this sort of arrangement.

By far the easiest, and most modern, way of finding a Sugar Daddy is online. There are a number of dedicated websites for this and at least everyone there knows what the deal is up front.

Some of the sites are:

www.seekingarrangement.com

www.sugardaddie.com

www.secretbenefits.com

www.sugardaddy.com

There are more niched sites than this as well, such as those for people looking to be paid per date or those who want to be taken on holiday, but as far as Sugar Daddy dating sites go, these are a good starting point. It's good to spread your bets by being on multiple sites, but do your research about each one before you commit. Some will charge, some won't, make sure you look at reviews before you spend.

These sites are just like specialised dating sites, you make a profile, search for your ideal partner and then message them through the site.

My method was purely online, I went with the top two Sugar Daddy websites at the time and made sure to check it for messages and new members regularly. Now there are a lot more sites out there, so I would not only go with a couple of the top sites but also sign up for those that would be specific for my needs.

How to set up a profile

Your profile is probably the most important thing to get you started on your sugar journey. As they say, first impressions are everything, and that can't be truer for Sugar Baby profiles. This is the first thing any potential Sugar Daddy will see and will be key to whether he is interested or not.

Different Sugar Daddies are after different things, so there isn't necessarily a right or wrong way to go about setting up a profile, but my biggest piece of advice is to keep it honest! How many times have you heard stories of people going on an online date only to find the person is nothing like their profile? The answer is probably too many! So, don't waste anyone's time by pretending to be something you're not able to live up to. You can present the best side of you, or a side that you want to explore with a Sugar Daddy, as long as you are not misleading. Unfortunately the world of sugar dating is competitive and the number of Sugar Babies well outnumbers the number of Sugar Daddies, so Sugar Daddies are not going to settle for someone they aren't happy with.

The persona you have on your profile is going to have to be the same as the one you can deliver in real life. Decide how you want to portray yourself and show off the best side of that. It's easiest to be you, be honest as you won't be able to keep up an act for long, so be your best possible self.

Let's start with photos. Photos are important, you are highly unlikely to find a Sugar Daddy if they can't see what you look like. Men will judge by the photos first, words second. Put a selection of photos on your profile, make them as glossy as possible of you by yourself. Sugar Daddies don't want to see photos of you with your friends on a night out (he doesn't need to be guessing which one is you), or you posing with a Snapchat filter. Think semi-professional, posed, take your time over these. Glamorous rather than slutty. Make the photos look good, but realistic, what they see in the photo should be what they get in real life. If you've put in a couple of good clear photos, then you can think about putting something additional, do you have a fun hobby that you could put a photo of? If you are all about travel then put a couple of photos of you in interesting locations? This is where some of your personality can show through as well.

Fill out as many sections of the profile as you can, being as detailed as possible. I'm going to say it again, the world of sugar dating is a competitive one! So give yourself the best possible chance by letting a Sugar Daddy find out who you are and what you can offer. Most Sugar Daddies are time poor, so don't want to play games trying to figure out if you are well suited. Use your words to show him you are worth spending time on and could be a long term Sugar Baby.

Let your personality shine through in the "About You" section. A Sugar Daddy can figure out quite quickly if you are a gold digger or someone worth spending their time/money on. Give them a glimpse of your background, your hobbies, what you do for fun, even your aspirations. Looks are important but conversation is too, so let potential Sugar Daddies know that you have layers!

It can be a good idea to lay out what your expectations are in terms of a sugar relationship, so write a line or two about what you are looking for in a Sugar Daddy and what the ideal scenarios are for you.

When writing a profile, be honest, give a good amount of detail, but remember to also stay safe. Don't put full names, too much detail of your location, exact places you work/study. Like in any aspect in life, there are always undesirables around, so be sure to keep yourself protected first and foremost.

When I started out, I was worried about posting my photos publicly. But I realised that even with a detailed profile description, I wasn't getting any replies. As soon as I put photos up things changed and I managed to get their attention! The great thing about some of the sites is that they have a section for private photos as well as public ones, so if you don't want to put too many photos up, you can also put some in a private album and only share access to the Sugar Daddies you are interested in.

First Contact

So you've uploaded some nice photos, written out a well thought out profile and it is live on the internet, that's the first big step complete!

The next step is finding potential Sugar Daddies. You can look through the potential Sugar Daddies on the site by using the search tool. It is a good idea to start by narrowing down by location as this is going to be one of the main factors, then going from there. You can search by age group, earnings, hair colour, ethnic background… as detailed as you desire!

You'll notice that many Sugar Daddies choose not to put photos on their profiles or even a decent amount of information. They can get away with this, Sugar Babies can't. That's because Sugar Daddies are so much more in demand. Unfortunately, this means that it can be a difficult search to find someone on the same wavelength as you, so you have to start shooting out messages in the dark to see who bites!

Make the first message simple and straight forward, introduce yourself and tell the Sugar Daddy why you have messaged them, what drew you to their profile? Make sure it's personalised to them, not just a generic message you send to 10 different people! It will make a world of difference and you will more likely get a reply.

Like all internet dating, you have to expect rejection, people not replying to your messages. Don't get too excited by someone's profile as you may never hear back from them. My best advice is to search for profiles you like the look of, send a message, then forget all about them. Then it is a bonus if you do hear back! The truth is, if a Sugar Daddy's profile looks perfect, then chances are you're not the only Sugar baby messaging him. You've got strong competition.

If you've got a great profile and a super opening message then hopefully a Sugar Daddy (or ten!) will get back to you. Of course it may be a Sugar Daddy that has found your profile and messages you first (winner!). Take the chance to message back and forth a few times to find out a little more about each other, talk about what you might have in common (spell out why YOU would be a great match). At this point it is a good idea to ask what the ideal arrangement would be for the Sugar Daddy, to see if this aligns with what you want.

If all is going well and you are both keen then usually at this stage you can exchange email addresses or phone numbers to get to know each other a bit more and even set up a first date. It can be wise to have an email address or sim card specifically for this purpose.

You will need a lot of patience to find a Sugar Daddy. There are a lot of profiles to sift through, trying to find someone you like to look of/sound of AND can offer you what you need can be tricky. Even when you find someone you may not even hear back from them. Persist and keep searching, someone will bite. You will probably have to go on quite a few first dates before you find the right Sugar Daddy. Keep on top of messages and reply promptly, check your spelling and grammar and avoid text speak!

Finding a Sugar Daddy is hard work! There are great Sugar Daddies out there, but they are hidden amongst profiles of men that don't check the site, fake profiles and time wasters. I spent a lot of time browsing through profiles and sending messages, for only a small percentage to reply, but in the long term the hard work was more than worthwhile.

The time wasters were the hardest. You know where you stand with people that just don't reply, but when someone messages you and tells you everything you want to hear only to never deliver, now that's frustrating! Who are these people? I will never know, but I presume they are not rich men, or people capable of being Sugar Daddies. They are probably people looking to get a bit of attention. My method is to try and organise a meeting/Skype call after only a few messages. But making the first messages count, by gleaming as much information as possible. A real Sugar Daddy won't want to be messaging back and forth for long either, that's not what they are there for and they just don't have the time.

CHAPTER 3

Dating

Setting the Rules/Allowances

So you've found a Sugar Daddy who seems to be on the same page as you and wants to take it further, what now? Well you need to establish the rules of this relationship, it is an arrangement after all!

You will need to have a discussion with your Sugar Daddy about how you will make this work, you need to establish the ground rules. For instance, is he married or in a high profile job which means that your meetings will have to be discrete? Is he time poor, so meetings can only be at certain times? Is he looking for someone to go for dinner with, shows, holidays, coffee…? How often, when, where and most importantly, what can he do for you?

The rules of Sugar Daddy dating are so fluid, that you just have to find an arrangement that works for you. Whether it is going on 2 dates a month and receiving £££ per date, or you becoming a travel partner, or receiving gifts as a part time 'girlfriend', the possibilities are endless, so keep an open mind to what your Sugar Daddy suggests. Talk it through and make sure the rules are clear.

My favourite type of arrangement was a combination of allowance and gifts. I would get a set amount per date and then also get treated, for example shopping trips and nights out. This seems to be one of the best arrangement in my eyes as Sugar Daddies love to be able to share the treat experience by splashing the cash for their Sugar Baby.

First date

For your first date/meeting make sure you meet in a public, safe space. Something as simple as a coffee date is best as it can be as long or short as you want it to be. Having dinner or going to an event can commit you to a long length of time, and if you quickly find out you don't like this Sugar Daddy, then things could get awkward!

Dress well for this meeting (and any subsequent dates). Look glamorous and alluring, don't look cheap and slutty. You should be someone he would be proud to have on his arm and someone that commands respect.

This is the time to find out if you are compatible, does the conversation flow, do your personalities match for the type of arrangement you're seeking? At this stage it really is about figuring out chemistry. If he brings up the details of the arrangement then it can be a good time to fine tune it, but at this stage I would avoid that to find out what you two as people are like together. If you're not gelling, then the likelihood is, this arrangement won't last.

Don't ask for money/gifts for a first date. This should be seen more like an interview for a job to find out if this arrangement could work. It will send red flags to the Sugar Daddy if you ask for something in exchange for this first meet up, as he will think you are only after money (gold digger!!) rather than having any interest in compatibility beyond that.

Early evening, cosy high-end bar, that is my favourite first meeting. It's relaxed and usually an environment like that can keep you pretty anonymous, which a Sugar Daddy loves. I would have only one alcoholic drink, then only Coca-Colas! I would never get drunk on a first date. I really believe in treating it like a two way interview. Stay professional, let them know what you bring to the table and let them woo you with what they bring. Check the tick boxes, does their profile ring true? Can they offer what you need? Is there chemistry between you?

The long term

A sugar arrangement can last a date or two, to many years. Like any relationship it can evolve over time as you get to know each other more and situations change. The long term of your arrangement is really down to you and your Sugar Daddy. But the important thing to remember is that this isn't a 'normal' relationship, it is an arrangement and you must both be aware of what that means and to make sure there is a defined set of rules that you have set out together, to make sure you both get out of the arrangement what you want and boundaries are made clear.

No matter how long the arrangement, you must stick to the rules you chose (unless you have had a conversation in which you both have agreed changes), but you must always deliver that persona you first promised. You can't get comfortable and start slacking, always look your best and be your best. This is business.

Talking of business, follow some rules as if this is a job. Turn up on time, don't cancel unless in an emergency, always be polite, stay well dressed. Don't give your Sugar Daddy a reason to get rid of you. On the flip side, a Sugar Daddy can get away with making changes, cancelling at last minute, it's just one of those things in sugar dating. They are the ones with busy schedules, families, so it is them that call the shots. As long as you are getting your allowance/gifts, that is all they are required to provide.

I've had Sugar Daddies that I've only been on a couple of dates with, to some I saw over many years. Each and every Sugar Daddy relationship was different and that's what I love about the lifestyle. I always made sure to stick to my side of the deal and respect my Sugar Daddies so my Sugar Daddies would do the same for me.

Discretion

Most Sugar Daddies will be most concerned about keeping things discrete. Let them contact you and let you know when is best to contact them, don't deviate from his rules. If he doesn't show up for a meeting or doesn't contact you, don't go chasing, there could be a very good reason he's gone MIA and that could be that someone might be figuring out what he is up to.

Keep your relationship between the two of you. Don't discuss specifics about him and your relationship with anyone else. Don't post photos of him on social media. Don't contact anyone around him. Stay professional!

Crossing the line

Okay let's put it out there. Two people, spending time together; dinner, dates, conversation… there's always a chance that someone will start getting feelings beyond that of a relationship. It happens. In rare cases the feelings might be reciprocated and the arrangement becomes a real relationship, fine, great! But (and this is a big BUT) this is an arrangement and the point of an arrangement is that you don't want/can't have a real relationship. This is first and foremost an agreement and a relationship second. So the likelihood is that if you develop feelings there is going to be big trouble. Don't do it. Don't let it happen. Keep yourself in check and remind yourself what this is all about. Treat this professionally.

If it happens, don't be surprised if your Sugar Daddy wants to end the relationship. Especially if he needs it to be discrete.

CHAPTER 4

Safety

Identities

I briefly touched on safety when talking about profiles, but feel that this is such an important topic that it needs it's own chapter.

Your safety must always come first! Be careful about revealing personal details. Your online profile should not have enough information that someone could track you down; don't list where you live, where you work, where you study. Don't list your full name or even your exact date of birth. There are a lot of great Sugar Daddies out there, but remember, like anywhere there are undesirables lurking. People who claim to be who they are not and you need to protect yourself against those types of people. People can play a good game, they can hold up a pretense for a long time, so even when you are dating someone use due diligence to protect yourself.

A lot of Sugar Babies like an allowance from their Sugar Daddies. But do you really want to give your bank details to a stranger? Probably not. There are other ways to receive money; cash, PayPal, pre-paid credit cards. Consider your options against your safety.

Sugar Daddies will also tend to play it safe with their identities. Some may not give their real name, or want to talk too much about their lives and what they do. This doesn't mean they are not genuine in what they want and can offer you. In fact this is pretty normal from a Sugar Daddy. Most Sugar Daddies want this type of arrangement as it is something that can be discrete and something very different from their normal lives, so they don't want the two to cross paths. They might be married, or in a high profile job, so won't want to reveal anything to you to keep their life safe. Don't take it personally, this is an arrangement after all and this is why you get something (money, gifts, business advice) out of it in return. If this bothers you then this isn't the lifestyle for you. Respect your Sugar Daddy and don't pry if he's not giving up details easily.

I would use my real first name but not give away my surname and I would talk about my work but not exactly where I worked, so I stayed honest but safe. As some of my relationships grew then my Sugar Daddies found out more about me, just as I did about them. But a trust is there that both sides would not take advantage of the information, we had an agreement between us, but beyond us we had no part in the others lives.

Internet Dating

Follow the same safety rules of internet dating. Alongside identity safety, you should also be making sure you look after yourself when meeting up with someone. Make your first meetings somewhere public. Let someone know where you are going and if they don't hear from you by a certain time, get them to check up on you. Don't feel pressured into doing anything you don't want, just because someone is giving you something doesn't mean you can't say NO!

So many fake profiles, too many! It has almost made me want to quit, but then BAM perfect Sugar Daddy comes along and saves the day just as I wanted to give up. If something hasn't sounded right, I've stopped talking to them. If when they turn up they are different from their profile, I won't take the dates any further. It's about self respect and recognising when someone might be taking advantage.

CHAPTER 5

Stigmas

Is it Prostitution?

A lot of people think that a Sugar Baby is basically an escort. Don't get me wrong, some people out there will be getting paid for sleeping with someone and label it a sugar relationship. But really it is a completely different arrangement and for many people, sex doesn't even come in to it.

A lot of Sugar Daddies are looking for companionship, someone to take to dinner, shows, the sort of things they would do with a girlfriend, but for whatever reason they don't have/want a girlfriend.

The Sugar Daddy/Sugar Baby arrangement isn't usually one off meet-ups, but rather a longer-term relationship. Sometimes things develop into a sexual relationship. But it doesn't have to. It is up to you if you want to have sex with someone! If you fancy your Sugar Daddy and things head that way and you are happy with it, great, go for it! If you just want a platonic relationship, also great, be honest, be open. A good Sugar Daddy will respect you and if he doesn't then maybe it isn't a Sugar Baby he needs…

Sex shouldn't be assumed, it should be a nice bonus for both of you if you do end up there! What you are getting out of the relationship shouldn't be related to whether you open your legs.

Just remember if you do, stay safe!

I've had sex with some of my Sugar Daddies, but that was because I WANTED to not HAD to. I wouldn't expect anything extra for it and it would have felt creepy if they had. I certainly didn't jump straight into bed with them and only did when it felt right and the chemistry had built to that moment.

Married Daddies

Probably one of the most common 'stigmas', Sugar Daddies are often married, with families. If this bothers you then this is not the path you should be following!

You have to look at this way, Sugar Babies are providing a service for married men. As couples marry, have kids, the man tends to feel less important. Like he blends in to the background and is only important for bringing in the money and fixing things round the house (okay, gender stereotypes, I know, it works both ways!). The excitement and attention he got from the relationship when it was new has faded. It doesn't mean he doesn't love his wife and kids, but it means his life is now lacking something. He doesn't want to leave them, he still wants to be married. An arrangement is perfect! He gets to date, go out, have some excitement and in turn his home life improves because he is still happy and still going back to the family he loves.

Just chat to Sugar Daddies, you will hear this time and time again. This isn't a bad thing, it doesn't make Sugar Daddies bad people.

The majority of my Sugar Daddies have been married and have been open about that fact. They've wanted me to know so that I understood the situation and the need for discretion. The married Sugar Daddies are often looking for the emotional connection, and are extremely kind and respectful. It was difficult to start with, to get my head around it all and whether I should feel guilty being 'the other woman'. But really that is not the role I was playing and ultimately I wasn't breaking their relationship, I was helping it by filling a part that was missing. So at the end of the day the Sugar Daddy returns home happier and home life is less stressful as he's not craving something.

Having Relationships

This is a tough one. Can you have a partner while being a Sugar Baby? The answer is that some people manage it, it is possible, but it is tricky. It is much easier to be a Sugar Baby when you are single, because a lot of things you do with a Sugar Daddy are the things you would do with someone you were dating (whether sex is involved or not). You are spending one on one time with someone, meeting up, chatting, forming a relationship. There is a huge risk of jealousy.

Also, from the Sugar Daddy perspective, a man likes to think he is the only guy in a woman's life. Hypocritical, yes, when they probably have a wife! But this is why you are getting allowances/gifts, to make up for the discretion he needs. A Sugar Daddy will often be put off knowing you are with someone else and not relying purely on them. This is also the reason that you should make a Sugar Daddy think he is the only Sugar Daddy you have, even if you are seeing more than one!

I've never tried this, nor wanted to. One of the main reasons I became a Sugar Baby is that I didn't want a 'real' relationship. Now that time has passed, I retired from being a Sugar Baby and settled down with my partner, I personally cannot see a way that I could still make the lifestyle work. The experiences I would be having with Sugar Daddies are the experiences I'd now rather be sharing with my partner.

Reliance on a Sugar Daddy

Having a Sugar Daddy can be a great way to get money, gifts, holidays, advice. Anything you can dream of! But it can be too easy to become reliant on them. This can be dangerous for two main reasons 1. You could be pushed to do things you don't want to do, to keep up the rewards and 2. If the Sugar Daddy stops the arrangement, you could be in trouble.

Make sure you are self-sufficient and can survive without your Sugar Daddy. Treat this as a bonus, not a living. Make sure you are always in control of yourself and have an alternative to him.

CHAPTER 6

The End of a Relationship

Don't Get Attached

Like all good things, a sugar relationship will come to an end. So, as well as not getting attached financially, don't get attached mentally! It can be a good idea to treat being a Sugar Baby like a business, you are providing a service to which you are being paid (gifted/treated..). If you start becoming too attached and even falling in love you are destined to get hurt.

The end of a sugar relationship should be able to be clear cut at any point, you should have no reliance on your Sugar Daddy, so if he disappears then there should be no big affect on you.

A Respectful End

There are many reasons for the relationship to end, but when it does, you must just accept it and move on. A Sugar Daddy might have decided he no longer needs a Sugar Baby, perhaps he wants a change of scenery, it doesn't matter. To be honest there shouldn't even need to be a reason, so don't go chasing him to find out. Accept and move on, be respectable.

You may be the one who wants to end the relationship. Again, be respectful. Be polite and let the Sugar Daddy know you are ending the arrangement. Don't just ghost him, thank him for his time and gifts. Let him know you appreciate what he has done for you.

All of my relationships with Sugar Daddies have ended amicably, the most common reason is that the relationships have just naturally run their course and it was time to move on. Things change, people change, what worked at the start may longer be suitable a few years down the line. I made sure never to close a door though.

Don't Ruin it for Everyone Else

Why be respectful? Well really it is for the greater good. So Sugar Babies can continue and thrive. Don't ruin it for everyone else!

If a Sugar Daddy has a bad experience, for example a clingy Sugar Baby, one that won't accept a 'break up', someone that stalks them. They won't want another Sugar Baby, the trust has been broken and the point of having the Sugar Baby has become void. The point of an arrangement is it isn't a commitment, it is easy to get into and out of and the Sugar Daddy is guaranteeing that by giving gifts/allowance. You are being paid to be discrete and really to be disposable to some degree.

Such a big community has been built of Sugar Babies and Sugar Daddies. It has been built on trust and success of previous arrangements. Anything that ends badly will tarnish the community and will put people off, meaning the days of the Sugar Baby could end.

CHAPTER 7

Conclusion

So that's it, everything you need to know to get started in the Sugar Baby world! It can be such a fun and rewarding world to be a part of, the possibilities can be endless! Every sugar relationship is unique and Sugar Babies all over the world have reaped unimaginable rewards. Remember stay honest, stay safe and most of all have fun!

My days as a Sugar Baby were so varied, so exciting. I loved meeting Sugar Daddies, I loved the chase and I loved the long-term experiences with them. There was never a dull moment, 'real' relationship stuff never got in the way, it was always like a new fresh relationship with no responsibilities.

I feel that Sugar Babies can get such a bad reputation, but the world is gradually opening their eyes and realising what a Sugar relationship really entails and how it can be as normal as any other relationship. I hope that by reading this guide you can gain the confidence to take those first steps and open up a world of opportunities. Good luck!

Printed in Great Britain
by Amazon